The BreakThrough Series

SMALL BOOKS | BIG CHANGE

A Life God
REWARDS

BRUCE WILKINSON
with DAVID KOPP

Multnomah®Publishers *Sisters, Oregon*

A LIFE GOD REWARDS
published by Multnomah Publishers, Inc.

© 2002 by Exponential, Inc.
International Standard Book Number: 1-57673-976-7

Cover design by David Carlson Design

Italics in Scripture quotations are the author's emphasis.

Scripture is from *The Holy Bible,* New King James Version.
Copyright © 1982 by Thomas Nelson, Inc. Used by permission.

Other Scripture quotations:
The Holy Bible, New International Version (NIV)
© 1973, 1984 by International Bible Society,
used by permission of Zondervan Publishing House

Multnomah is a trademark of Multnomah Publishers, Inc.,
and is registered in the U.S. Patent and Trademark Office.
The colophon is a trademark of Multnomah Publishers, Inc.

Printed in the United States of America

For information:
MULTNOMAH PUBLISHERS, INC. • P.O. BOX 1720 • SISTERS, OR 97759

Library of Congress Cataloging-in-Publication Data:
Wilkinson, Bruce.
  A life god rewards / by Bruce Wilkinson.
      p. cm.
   ISBN 1-57673-976-7
 1. Future life—Christianity.   I. Title.
   BT903 .W55 2002
   236'.2—dc21

                                                         2002009394

         02 03 04 05 06 07 08—10 9 8 7 6 5 4 3 2 1 0

TABLE OF CONTENTS

*For those who might be wondering
today if God notices or cares.*

*I'm especially grateful to Don Jacobson for his
personal commitment to this project from its inception.
My thanks also to the whole Multnomah team,
especially to Jennifer Gott, Steffany Woolsey,
Bill Jensen, and Guy Coleman for their outstanding
support. And as always to my writing partner, David
Kopp, and our editor, Heather Harpham Kopp,
my deepest appreciation and respect.*

PREFACE

Dear Reader,

You're about to encounter the teachings of Jesus on a very surprising subject—the direct connection between what you do today and what you will experience in eternity.

Jesus revealed that two truths determine our eternal experience. Think of them as keys. The first key is belief—what you believe determines your eternal destination.

But what is the second key? What treasure from God does it unlock? And why did Jesus talk so much about it?

That is the subject of this book.

Jesus is recognized around the world and in every religion as a great teacher. Yet millions of people today, including a majority of His followers, do not seem to have heard what He said about a life God rewards. Have you?

The message of this little book has the potential to transform what you expect from God and what you will deeply desire to do for Him, starting today. I hope you read it prayerfully and expectantly.

Warmly,
Bruce Wilkinson

1

KEYHOLE TO THE STARS

"Rejoice in that day and leap for joy!

For indeed your reward is great in heaven."

JESUS, IN LUKE 6:23

What if today really *was* the first day of the rest of your life? Today you make your trade—everything you have accomplished and become for whatever God offers in exchange. There you are, poised on the brink, lifetime in hand, ready to step into eternity.

What a moment! And what an amazing exchange! Your blink in the sun for God's endless day. Your spoonful of water for His Amazon River.

You take your step. You put down your little handful of time and pick up your forever life....

No one made more shocking statements about the afterlife than Jesus.

But what if I told you that the small choices you make today—like how you interact with your boss, or whom you invite to dinner—could change what happens next?

Would you be surprised?

In the little book you're holding, you're going to discover that Jesus revealed that our actions now will affect our future forever. Astoundingly, millions who follow Jesus seem to have missed what He said.

Could you be one?

I was. I grew up in a family that attended church regularly, and I was taught the Bible from the time I was young. Later I spent nine years pursuing theological training. But the clear teachings of Jesus on this subject remained lost to me, like overlooked treasures in my own house. When I finally discovered them, many things started to make sense for the first time.

Let's admit it: Any change in how we think about our future, even if it could radically improve our prospects, takes courage. We struggle to let go of comfortable assumptions, even when they're preventing us from seeing the whole truth. We're like toddlers peering through a keyhole at the night sky, trying to hold on to our tiny patch of stars.

But the keyhole is so small and the view is so great. Jesus wants to open the door and show us more.

Much more.

PREPARE TO BE ASTONISHED

No one made more shocking statements about the afterlife than Jesus of Nazareth. His teachings often left His audiences amazed, dumbfounded, even outraged. Take His first public appearance at the age of twelve: "All who heard Him were astonished at His understanding and answers" (Luke 2:47).

When Jesus formally began His ministry, His audience was again "astonished" (Matthew 7:28). In His teaching known as the Sermon on the Mount, Jesus said:

> *"Blessed are you when men hate you,*
> *   And when they exclude you,*
> *And revile you, and cast out your name as evil,*
> *   For the Son of Man's sake.*
> *Rejoice in that day and leap for joy!"*
>
> LUKE 6:22–23

You might know these verses well. I have to confess that I read them dozens, if not scores, of times before I *really* read them. Jesus' statement seems incredible, doesn't it? I used to think He was saying something like, "If you are persecuted on My behalf, you'll be so happy that you'll jump for sheer delight."

But if you read on, it's clear that that's not what Jesus meant. He continued:

"For indeed your reward is great in heaven."

v. 23

In those eight words, Jesus reveals why you and I can rejoice, even in the worst circumstances. Why? Because there is a direct connection between something you do for Him on earth and something "great" He will do for you in heaven.

Notice that Jesus describes it as a reward for *doing*, which would distinguish it, for example, from a gift you receive for *believing*. Also, the reward is specifically and personally yours if you behave in one way, but is not yours if you behave in another (for example, if you ran away under the pressure of persecution).

You see, Jesus *isn't* asking you and me to enjoy misery on His behalf. Instead He's saying that the consequences in heaven for certain actions on earth will be so wonderful that simply knowing they're coming—and knowing that they will be great—can transform how we live now. Yes, and even create spontaneous outbursts of joy!

This promise of reward in heaven isn't an isolated example of Jesus' teachings on the subject:

- "He will *reward* each according to his works" (Matthew 16:27).
- "You will have *treasure* in heaven" (Matthew 19:21).
- "You will be blessed...for you shall be *repaid* at the resurrection" (Luke 14:14).

As you're about to discover, the implications of these passages are enormous. For one thing, they suggest that God is keeping track of what you do for Him every day. For another, that you have more to gain by serving Him than you ever imagined.

TRACKING DOWN THE PROMISE

Let me tell you how I came to write this book. In 1985 when I first stumbled upon Jesus' teachings on reward in heaven, I was startled. What He was saying seemed to contradict much of what I had always been taught and believed.

So I began an intensive search for the truth, starting with every Bible verse on the subject of eternal rewards. I studied theological and scholarly works. I spent hours thinking about what Jesus seemed to be saying with such urgency. And I became convinced that spiritual seekers around the world, including millions of Jesus' followers, had mislaid a truth of great importance and promise—and it was time to get it back.

Five years of in-depth study and twelve thick binders later, my findings lined the shelves of my study.

One day I got a call from Dr. Earl Radmacher, president of Western Seminary in Oregon, inviting me to present my material in a weeklong graduate course at the seminary. I agreed, but only after he promised to assemble a panel of leading scholars, including some who had also been studying rewards, to sit in and evaluate every word.

On an April morning several months later, I walked across the seminary campus, lugging my teaching materials. I arrived at the lecture room, which was filled with some of the brightest individuals I had ever met: department chairpersons of the Greek and Hebrew languages, church historians, Bible teachers, seminarians, and pastors from a range of denominations.

I taught every morning for four hours. Each afternoon, a special group of scholars met at Dr. Radmacher's home and debated every point.

What Jesus was saying seemed to contradict much of what I had always believed.

One day a church historian from Romania assured us that what we were studying was not new theology; it had been part of Christian beliefs and teaching from the first century on. To make his point he asked us, "What do the greats of church history such as Augustine, Luther, Calvin, Wesley, and Spurgeon all have in common?"

When everyone hesitated, he told us his answer: "They all earnestly believed in and hoped for eternal rewards."

We'll carefully construct the biggest, truest view posssible of your entire life.

Toward the end of the week, I noticed a shift. The roomful of scholars was spending less time debating and more time responding personally to the material. One afternoon an older participant pulled me aside. "I thought God brought me here to learn more about eternal rewards," he said, "but I was wrong. He brought me here to change my heart—I'm leaving a changed professor!"

On the last day, I asked the group, "Are you convinced that what I've been teaching about rewards is consistent with what Jesus taught?"

"We're convinced," they replied. And I have never looked back.

THE TWO KEYS

In the pages ahead, you'll encounter for yourself the findings we explored that week at Western Seminary. Whether you're familiar with Jesus' teachings about eternal rewards or you're coming upon them for the first time, I encourage you to read with great expectation. Important spiritual breakthroughs await you.

Starting with statements Jesus made, we'll carefully construct the biggest, truest view possible of your entire life. We'll be using a lot of familiar words—words like *heaven, treasure, works,* and *faith.* I urge you to be patient as we look beneath these familiar labels for hidden insights.

The teachings of Jesus show us that there are two keys that determine everything about your eternity.

The first key is your *belief.* This key unlocks the door to eternal life and determines *where* you will spend eternity.

The second key is your *behavior.* It unlocks the door to reward and determines *how* you will spend eternity.

This second key is the focus of *A Life God Rewards.* Although the role of behavior (we'll also use words like *actions* or *works*) isn't more important to your future than belief, it has been more overlooked in recent times. And the promise of rediscovering the truths it unlocks is enormous, especially for followers of Jesus.

In fact, by the time you're done reading, you'll

approach daily life in a dramatically different way. Simple decisions, such as how you spend your time and money, will become opportunities of great promise. And you will begin to live with an unshakable certainty that everything you do today matters forever.

RUMORS OF BLUE WHALES

In the first book in this series, *The Prayer of Jabez,* we learned that God wants us to ask for His blessing and for greater influence, or "territory," in this world. The next book, *Secrets of the Vine,* showed that Jesus wants our territory to produce a great harvest of good works for Him.

You will begin to live with an unshakable certainty that everything you do today matters forever.

In *A Life God Rewards,* I want to show you how the harvest you produce will directly impact your experience in eternity— and how that truth can change your life today for the better.

I'll admit that on a subject like eternity, we must proceed thoughtfully and humbly. We're

16

like tadpoles swapping stories of blue whales. We're like one twin in the womb trying to convince his brother that it's only a matter of time before they're both breathing air and riding tricycles.

Fortunately for all of us, God sent His Son from heaven to help us see the whole truth. If you and I are willing to be surprised, unsettled, even shocked by His words, our prospects for living a life He rewards will change for the better, starting now.

2

THE UNBREAKABLE LINK

"For the Son of Man will come in the
glory of His Father with His angels,
and then He will reward each
according to his works."

JESUS, IN MATTHEW 16:27

Blink.
That's the first thing you'll notice—simply no transition. No bridge from temporary to eternal. No gradual awakening. No strolling toward heaven through a long corridor of light (where you might, for example, rethink your direction and decide to go back). No spare moment to decide that, yes, it finally is time to consider what God said.

You will go from instant to instant. One instant, earth; the next, eternity.…

Blink.

And then what?

If you're like most people, you picture eternity somewhat like a West Texas highway—flat, long, and monotonous. You expect that after your death all the big events of your life will be behind you.

But Jesus reveals something else entirely. As the only person to come from eternity to earth, then return to eternity, Jesus knows the whole truth— past, present, and future—and can give you a one-of-a-kind perspective. For example, He can see your present (there you are, reading *A Life God Rewards*) from a moment far out in your infinite future and tell you exactly how to prepare for what is to come.

Most people picture eternity somewhat like a West Texas highway—flat, long, and monotonous.

Listen to a moment in the future that Jesus told His disciples about:

> *"For the Son of Man will come in the glory of His Father with His angels, and then He will reward each according to his works."*
>
> MATTHEW 16:27

Jesus was describing a specific series of events in every believer's future that will alter our experience of eternity: He will come again, He will bring rewards, and His rewards will be given to "each according to his works." Since Jesus hasn't yet come again, we can conclude that even His disciples are still waiting in heaven for the event Jesus described in this verse.

Does this news surprise you?

If so, you will appreciate what comes next. To help you get the most out of what Jesus wants you to know about His rewards, we're going to start with the big picture first. In this chapter, we'll step back from the keyhole, let Jesus open the door, and get a big Milky Way view of every person's future.

And you'll understand how the long line of your future is being decided by one little dot called today.

THE (REAL) TIMELINE OF YOUR ETERNITY

If we look closely at what Jesus said, we discover that our eternal life has a clear and knowable timeline of events. In fact, Jesus revealed that most of our life happens *after* our physical death.

The timeline that follows focuses on events that

will happen to you in the future. Jesus talked about these events often. And they apply to you no matter what your religion or what choices you're making today about your beliefs or actions.

We'll get more details later, but for now, think of the timeline as a road map to your future with only the main intersections marked.

THE SIX MAIN EVENTS
OF YOUR FOREVER LIFE

1. LIFE. *You are created in the image of God for a life of purpose.*

Let's start with now. Although you didn't exist forever in the past, you will continue to exist forever in the future. Between birth and death, you live on earth as a body, soul, and spirit (John 3:6; 4:23–24; 1 Thessalonians 5:23).

2. DEATH. *You die physically, but not spiritually.*

Just as birth is your brief entrance into life on earth, so the death of your body is your instantaneous exit. Yet since you are more than organic matter, your life as soul and

A LIFE GOD REWARDS

spirit continues. Neither reincarnation nor "soul sleep" is taught in the Bible. Jesus revealed that after death your soul is either with God in heaven or apart from God in hell (Luke 23:43; 2 Corinthians 5:8).

3. DESTINATION. *You reach your destination after death, which is determined by what you believed on earth.*

Your eternal destination is decided by whether you believed in Jesus while you were still alive (John 3:16–18). In all of His teaching, Jesus identified only two possible locations in the afterlife: heaven or hell (John 14:2; Matthew 23:33). Both last forever.

4. RESURRECTION. *You receive a resurrected body.*

In eternity, every person will experience bodily resurrection (John 5:28–29). Our new bodies will be immortal—they can never again experience death (1 Corinthians 15). For those who are resurrected to life, Jesus "will transform our lowly body that it may be conformed to His glorious body" (Philippians 3:21).

5. REPAYMENT. *You receive your reward or your retribution for eternity based on what you did on earth.*

Although your eternal destination is based on your belief, how you spend eternity is based on your behavior while on earth. Believers and nonbelievers will be judged by Jesus Christ at events called the bema and the great white throne (John 5:22; 2 Corinthians 5:10; Revelation 20:11–15). The outcome will determine your degree of reward in heaven or retribution in hell (Matthew 11:21–22; 23:14).

6. ETERNITY. *You will live forever in the presence or absence of God, reaping the consequences of your beliefs and actions on earth.*

Jesus taught that an eternal existence awaits everyone. Those who have rejected Him "will go away into everlasting punishment," while those who have chosen Him will experience eternal life in God's presence (Matthew 25:46). The eternity that Jesus reveals is not just an existence or state of mind, but a real life in a real place.

❦

If you're already familiar with what the Bible says about future events, you may have noticed that some were not included, such as the Rapture, the Second Coming of Jesus, the Tribulation, and the Kingdom. That's because we've tried to describe a broad view of the events everyone will experience.

MAKE THE CONNECTION

Even a whirlwind tour of eternity shows just how much is at stake in what lies ahead for you. Clearly your future according to Jesus holds great promise for fulfillment and reward—if you make certain choices now.

Which brings us to a connection that many miss. Maybe you've already seen it.

If you look at the six main events of your forever life in terms of cause and effect, you'll notice that your life now is directly impacting everything that will happen to you after you die. Between your life on earth and every later event in your life, there is an invisible, one-way connection.

I describe this critical connection as the Law of the Unbreakable Link:

*Your choices on earth have direct
consequences on your life in eternity.*

Think of the Law of the Unbreakable Link like the law of gravity—it's always present, always working, even when you can't see it and even if you don't believe it. The choices you make in your life don't come to nothing when you die. They matter. And they will continue to matter throughout eternity!

*Your future holds
great promise
for fulfillment
and reward—
if you make certain
choices now.*

When we study the events of our timeline, we see that there are really two sets of consequences (I described them as keys in chapter 1):

- Our eternal destination is the consequence of what we believe on earth.
- Our eternal compensation is the consequence of how we behave on earth.

I grew up understanding only part of what the link shows. I knew that what I believed on earth would affect where I spent eternity. But I assumed that my actions (once the issue of my belief was resolved) would not have a direct consequence on what heaven would be like for me. You can see that I applied the link to my faith but not to my actions.

Let me ask you, do you believe your choices today *are* directly linked to what you will experience in your eternity?

Jesus came to show you how you can change your future, beginning with one small choice.

It's been my observation that people all over the world fall into one of two camps on this issue. One camp emphasizes the consequence of beliefs on an individual's eternal future and tends to minimize the importance of works. The other camp emphasizes the consequence of good works on an individual's eternal future and tends to minimize the issue of belief.

Each camp tends to look down on the other—and, unfortunately, sees only part of the big picture.

Do these observations ring true in your experience?

And let me ask you: Which consequence of the link may have slipped from view in your thinking?

Consider what rediscovering the connection between your life now and your life in eternity could mean for you. If your actions today *do* have the potential to radically affect your eternity, wouldn't that dramatically change how you think about your life? How you think about God? What you choose to do one minute from now?

Jesus wants you to know that the positive consequences of your actions and beliefs today can change your eternity in astounding and wonderful ways—and He doesn't want you to waste another minute believing otherwise.

You don't need to wonder or worry about what might await you on the other side of your last heartbeat. In His great mercy, Jesus came to earth from eternity so you could know exactly what consequences your actions and beliefs will have there.

And because He came, eternity need hold no threat, only great promise.

THE DOT AND THE LINE

I want to show you a picture that will help you keep the reality of the unbreakable link at the forefront of your thinking as you make your daily choices.

Below you see a dot and a line. The dot is small and exists in one little place. The line begins in one place, then takes off across the page. Imagine that the line extends off the page and goes on and on, without end.

•————————————————————————————————————→

The dot stands for your whole life here on earth. For most of us, that's about seventy years.

The line represents your life after death in eternity. That's forever and ever.

As we saw in our timeline, Jesus' teaching shows that *what happens inside the dot determines everything that happens on the line.* Even a small choice in the dot can result in a corresponding consequence on the line of astounding proportions.

Whenever audiences grasp this mental picture, their reactions are immediate and intense. They say things like, "If this is true, it changes everything for me!" Or, "I can't believe I've prepared for my children's future and my old age without giving a thought to my *real* future!" One man said to me, "I've always thought about finishing well, but it turns out that death is just the starting gate!"

You don't need to wonder or worry about what might await you on the other side of your last heartbeat.

Can you identify with any of these reactions? Would you say you've been living for the line or for the dot?

If your answer is the latter, your prospects are about to look up. Jesus came to show you how you can change your future, beginning with one small choice.

Just ask a group of dinner guests....

3

WHAT THE BIBLE SAYS
ABOUT REWARDS

"When you give a feast, invite the poor, the maimed,

the lame, the blind. And you will be blessed,

because they cannot repay you; for you shall be

repaid at the resurrection of the just."

JESUS, IN LUKE 14:13–14

I t happened one Sabbath. Jesus, along with a distinguished list of guests, had been invited to dinner at the home of a prominent leader (Luke 14:1). As the guests were finding their places, Jesus watched them jockey for the best seats.

Suddenly, He offered some unsolicited advice:

"Sit down in the lowest place.... For whoever exalts himself will be humbled, and he who humbles himself will be exalted."

Everywhere, power players flinched. But Jesus wasn't finished. He turned to the host and proceeded to instruct him on a better way to entertain guests:

> *"When you give a dinner or a supper, do not ask your friends, your brothers, your relatives, nor rich neighbors, lest they also invite you back, and you be repaid."*

v. 12

What an awkward moment! Jesus seemed to be saying to His host, "Next time, don't invite all these people you invited tonight."

Was He questioning the man's taste in friends or his grasp of social etiquette? Look closely at what Jesus said next:

> *"When you give a feast, invite the poor, the maimed, the lame, the blind. And you will be blessed."*

vv. 13–14

Rather than criticizing His host for his generosity, Jesus was showing him how to get something

That evening, Jesus had something else in mind.

important—something more lasting than a wonderful evening—in exchange for it. The first hint we get of that something is in the word *blessed*.

Blessed! All of us know that feeling. My family experienced it one day when we pulled off the highway for lunch and decided to buy a meal for a homeless traveler sitting outside the restaurant. When my daughter presented him with the biggest cheeseburger on the menu, he beamed at her with a toothless smile, and we made a new friend.

I still remember how I felt as our car pulled back onto the interstate. Completely rewarded. All-over warm. Yes, Jesus was right. Blessings do come when you do good deeds to those who cannot repay you.

But that's not what Jesus was talking about.

That evening, Jesus had something else in mind.

WHAT JESUS SAID NEXT

The rest of Jesus' statement brings us to the heart of the Bible's teaching on rewards:

"And you will be blessed, because they cannot repay you; for you shall be repaid at the resurrection of the just."

v. 14

No one in the room could have missed Jesus' astonishing revelation—God will repay you for a good work *after you are dead.* This contradicts what most people believe today and what everyone in that room believed—that God rewards people only on earth for the good they do in this life.

Jesus revealed just the opposite. His words show that when you do a worthy deed for a person who cannot repay you:

1. You will be repaid.
2. Your payment will come in the next life.
3. When you receive it, you will be blessed.

Certainly, God blesses us here on earth out of His unmerited grace and goodness. God may also give us temporal rewards for right choices or faithful service to Him in the here and now. But the rewards Jesus reveals in this story—and the ones He talks about most—are different. They are God's guaranteed response to a specific action on our part that will continue to affect our lives far into eternity. These rewards come not from asking, but from doing—and not now, but after death.

Miss these differences and you set yourself up for disappointment. You'll find yourself asking questions like these: *I serve God in every way I know how, so why is our family struggling so much financially? Doesn't God notice or care?* Friend, God notices and cares. But He doesn't promise that work for Him now will always result in gain from Him now.

In fact, the rewards Jesus wanted you and me to know about most do *not* come now. He said it in His first sermon, and he said it again to a roomful of religious know-it-alls at dinner....

His eternal rewards come later, and they begin with something you do today.

WHAT DOES JESUS MEAN BY *REWARD?*

Interestingly, the Bible uses two different words to describe Jesus' reward.

The Greek word used in Jesus' teachings in Luke 6 is *misthos*. Literally, it means *wages:* "Rejoice in that day and leap for joy! For indeed your *misthos* [wages] are great in heaven" (Luke 6:23).

Jesus used the same word later when He spoke of earthly wages: "Call the laborers and give them their *misthos* [wages]" (Matthew 20:8). And Paul told Timothy, "The laborer is worthy of his *misthos* [wages]" (1 Timothy 5:18).

Everyone who heard Jesus understood exactly what He meant: "When you labor on earth, your employer gives you *misthos*. And when you labor for Me, I pay you wages, too."

Jesus' rewards begin with something you do today.

Jesus never described His reward as a charitable tip ("Here's a little something extra"), or a token of appreciation (like a plaque for thirty years at the factory). He called it wages—something you earn resulting from something you do.

The second word used for reward in heaven

appears in our dinner story in this chapter. Here Jesus used a compound word, *apodidomai*. *Apo* means *back,* and *didomai* means *to give*. Combined, *apodidomai* means to give back in return, or simply, repay:

> *"You will be blessed...for you shall be* apodidomai *[given back in return] at the resurrection of the just."*
>
> LUKE 14:14

Jesus also used this term in His well-known story about the Good Samaritan, who stopped to help a traveler that had been beaten and robbed by bandits. When the Samaritan took the injured man to a nearby inn for care, he told the innkeeper, "Take care of him; and whatever more you spend, when I come again, I will *apodidomai* [repay] you" (Luke 10:35).

The word *apodidomai* takes the idea of wages into even more surprising territory. Jesus says that when you receive His *apodidomai*, you are being reimbursed in full measure for what you did on His behalf. If you're thinking that God would repay you only for grand acts of personal sacrifice and not everyday acts of love, remember that Jesus said, "For whoever gives you a cup of water to drink in My name…will by no means lose his *apodidomai* [repayment]" (Mark 9:41).

Have you heard and embraced Jesus' amazing promise? No deed for God will pass by overlooked or unrewarded. Not one cup of water, or one prayer in the middle of the night.

Jesus never described His reward as a charitable tip.

PORTRAIT OF A LIFE

I visited recently with a bedridden elderly woman named Vera. "I get so discouraged lying here all day, Dr. Wilkinson," she said. "I can't really *do* anything for God but pray."

"Do you pray a lot?" I asked.

Vera thought for a minute before replying. "Oh, for half of my day, I suppose. And some of the night, too."

I encouraged Vera by reminding her that Jesus said private prayer is so valuable to God that "your Father who sees in secret will reward you openly" (Matthew 6:6).

Maybe, like Vera, you're doing more of eternal value than you realize. So what would a portrait of a life God rewards look like?

Nowhere does Jesus give an exhaustive list of what actions He will reward. Yet I've observed in cultures around the world that people know instinctively what a good work is—an act you do for someone that meets a need and honors God. In *Secrets of the Vine,* we saw how much God wants and works for this kind of fruitfulness in every person's life. Jesus told His disciples, "By this My Father is glorified, that you bear much fruit" (John 15:8).

Maybe you're doing more of eternal value than you realize.

We see a vivid picture of the life God rewards in the teachings of Jesus and in the rest of the New Testament. To help you remember this portrait of a life God rewards, I've used words beginning with *S.* Vera is a good example of the first *S:*

1. God will reward you for *seeking* Him through spiritual acts such as fasting and praying (Matthew 6:6; Hebrews 11:6).

2. God will reward you for *submitting* to your employer as a faithful steward (Matthew 24:45–47; Ephesians 6:8; Colossians 3:22–24).

3. God will reward you for *self-denial* in His service (Matthew 16:24–27).

4. God will reward you for *serving* those in need in His name (Mark 9:41).

5. God will reward you for *suffering* for His name and reputation (Luke 6:22–23).

6. God will reward you for *sacrifices* you make for Him (Luke 6:35). In fact, Jesus said that every person who sacrifices to follow Him will be rewarded a hundredfold (Matthew 19:29)!

7. God will reward you for *sharing* of your time, talent, and treasure to further His kingdom (Matthew 6:3–4; 1 Timothy 6:18–19).

As you read this list, you might see areas where you have already made a priority of doing what God promises to reward. Or you might read the list and feel discouraged: *This looks like the description of a supersaint like Billy Graham or Mother Teresa. How could someone like me possibly earn rewards?*

Let me reassure you. In the pages to come, you're going to see that every person on earth, regardless of circumstance or ability, has an equal opportunity to please God and receive His "Well done, good and faithful servant" (Matthew 25:21).

GOD'S PREROGATIVE

I've noticed that people who are making these discoveries for the first time respond with a wide range of feelings. Some experience intense gratitude; some, a burst of anticipation. But others tell me they are reluctant to believe what they're hearing. They'll say, "But I don't deserve any reward!" Or, "If I'm spending eternity with Jesus in heaven, why would I want or need anything more?"

I couldn't believe that God would want to reward me for what I was already willingly doing for Him.

I understand these feelings. I had them myself when I first explored this topic. In fact, I didn't agree with God's plan at all! I'd been happily working for God for years. I couldn't believe that God would want to reward me for what I was already willingly doing for Him. After all, Jesus died for me. Serving Him was the least I could do for Him!

Two passages in the Gospels helped my thinking begin to change:

- In Luke 17:10, Jesus told His disciples: "When you have done all those things which you are commanded, say, 'We are unprofitable servants. We have done what was our duty to do.'"

This passage shows that, above all, it is my duty and privilege to serve God. If Jesus thanks me, it is because He is gracious and generous, not because I am deserving.

- In Matthew 20:1–16, Jesus told a parable about laborers who worked different lengths of time but all received the same wages. At the end of the day, when the workers who had worked all day questioned the landowner's fairness, he said, "Is it not lawful for me to do what I wish with my own things? Or is your eye evil because I am good?" (v. 15).

This second passage reminds me that God can be as generous as He wants with what belongs to Him. If I argue with His amazing goodness, it may be because goodness is lacking in my own heart.

Then one day I reencountered a familiar verse that changed my thinking on this matter once and for all.

MEET THE REWARDER

You'll find this verse in Hebrews, nestled in a passage about heroes who pleased God with their faith. "Without faith it is impossible to please Him," the writer says, "for he who comes to God must believe that He is, and that He is a *rewarder*" (11:6).

If you look up that word *rewarder* in the Greek, you'll be amazed by what you discover. The word used here is neither *misthos* nor *apodidomai,* but an unusual combination of both. In fact, Hebrews 11:6 is the only verse in the Bible where you'll find it used to describe a person. God is the *misthos-apodidomai*—the rewarder who pays back your wages in return.

You see, God chooses to reward because it is an expression of His own generous nature. His plan to reward, like His provision to save, is a display of His amazing grace.

And there's no other way to think about it. The Bible says if you want to please God, you *must* believe that "He is," but you also *must* believe something else. That your God "is a rewarder."

Today, this takes faith. But in the next chapter I'll take you to the day in your future when Jesus will prove it to you face-to-face.

"He who comes to God must believe that He... is a rewarder."

4

THAT DAY

"For the Father judges no one,

but has committed all judgment to the Son,

that all should honor the Son

just as they honor the Father."

JESUS, IN JOHN 5:22–23

H ave you ever sat, eyes glued to the television, watching the Olympic awards ceremonies with tears streaming down your cheeks?

I have. There's something about the scene that pulls at a person's heart.

Your favorite athlete climbs the steps of the awards platform, her national anthem fills the stadium, her nation's flag waves in the spotlight. Her years of sweat and self-denial have paid off. She has finished her race. And she has won.

Now, as thousands applaud, an Olympic official drapes a medal around her neck.

One day you and I will have our own awards ceremony in eternity. The halls of heaven will ring with praise and celebration. Witnesses from every nation and every generation will watch with eager anticipation. Even angels will pause....

Because our race of faith will be done. The moment will have arrived for us to stand at the platform and receive our reward.

On that day, who do you think will be our judge and rewarder?

One day you and I will have our own awards ceremony in eternity.

The best judge would be a person who understands complete justice from heaven's perspective but who also knows what it feels like to live in the heat and dust and discouragement of everyday life.

Only Jesus could be the One. The Bible says He was "in all points tempted as we are, yet without sin" (Hebrews 4:15). And in fact, the Bible says Jesus *will* be our judge. Jesus Himself announced to His disciples that the authority to judge had been given to Him by God:

> *"For the Father judges no one, but has committed all judgment to the Son."*
>
> JOHN 5:22

Paul, thinking ahead to his own awards ceremony, wrote: "There is laid up for me the crown of righteousness, which the Lord, the righteous Judge, will give to me on that Day, and not to me only but also to all who have loved His appearing" (2 Timothy 4:8).

Do you look forward to meeting your Savior in person? Then this chapter is especially for you. We will look more deeply into Event 5: Repayment.

We'll begin by giving you a picture of what you will experience when you stand before Jesus to receive His repayment for what you did in your life on earth. Remember, everyone will give an account, and everyone will receive compensation from God based on his works. When the apostle Paul wrote to churches, he referred to a judgment at the bema of

Jesus. The apostle John wrote about a judgment at a great white throne.

In the next few minutes, we're going to answer some important questions about that wonderful occasion: How will Jesus evaluate what we did for Him? What could we gain or lose? And how will we respond?

No one wrote in more detail about that day than the apostle Paul, perhaps because he experienced an unexpected preview of its significance one day in the Greek city of Corinth....

PAUL AT THE BEMA

Paul had been living in Corinth for several months, spreading the news of the gospel at every opportunity, when trouble hit. His enemies dragged him into court and charged him with "persuading the people to worship God in ways contrary to the law" (Acts 18:13, NIV).

Scholars believe that a raised marble platform still visible today in the ruins of Corinth is the exact place where the provincial magistrate sat to hear Paul's case. The platform was called the *bema*, which is the Greek word for *judgment seat*. The same word was applied to the place where officials sat at athletic contests. The bema represented authority, justice, and reward (John 19:13; Acts 25:10–12).

At Paul's hearing, he stood before a magistrate named Gallio while his enemies argued for his punishment. But when it came Paul's turn to defend himself, Gallio stopped the proceedings. He had already decided that no crime had occurred. Paul was free to go.

Considering the apostle's tumultuous life, the incident at the bema in Corinth was a mere blip.

Or was it?

Three years later, Paul sent a letter back to the church in Corinth. In it he talked about another bema, this one in heaven. He told them that every follower of Jesus would have an appointment there one day:

> For we must all appear before the judgment seat
> [bema] of Christ, that each one may receive the
> things done in the body, according to what he has
> done, whether good or bad.
>
> 2 CORINTHIANS 5:10

Notice two important phrases: When Paul writes "that each one may receive," he is clearly indicating a reward or repayment. And when he says "things done in the body," he is restricting the reward to things you did while you were alive on earth. As you know, this takes place in heaven after you die.

The scene that played out on the stones of Corinth gave Paul a compelling picture—one he wanted the church in Corinth to see and remember: We will all face the bema, we will all stand alone, and our judge will be Jesus Christ Himself.

SHOW AND TEST

Two years later, when Paul wrote to encourage the Christians in Rome, the bema came up again:

> *We shall all stand before the judgment seat [bema] of Christ.... Each of us shall give account of himself to God.*

ROMANS 14:10, 12

What did Paul mean by "give account"? A different visual description of our judgment, found in 1 Corinthians 3, gives some key insights. In it, Paul pictures not a platform but a building, which represents our works, undergoing a test by fire:

*Now if anyone builds on this foundation with gold,
silver, precious stones, wood, hay, straw, each one's
work will become clear; for the Day will declare it,
because it will be revealed by fire.*

vv. 12–13

*You aren't being
tested here. Your
beliefs aren't being
tested, either.*

We know from the previous verse that the foundation Paul refers to is Jesus. When put together, these verses clarify that the first purpose of the bema is to *show*. Notice the key words—*become clear, declare,* and *revealed.* At a time of accounting after Jesus comes (Paul, like Jesus, calls it "the Day"), all that we have done for God will be plainly and completely apparent.

A second purpose of the judgment at the bema is to *test* our works:

*The fire will test each one's work, of what sort it is.
If anyone's work which he has built on it endures,*

*he will receive a reward. If anyone's work is
burned, he will suffer loss; but he himself will be
saved, yet so as through fire.*

VV. 13–15

Notice that *you* aren't being tested here. *Your beliefs*
aren't being tested. And *your destination* in eternity isn't
being tested.

So what is tested at the bema? *Your works.* What
you did with your life will endure like gold, silver, and
precious stones in a fire. Or it will burn up like straw—
not a trace will remain, no matter how sensible,
enjoyable, or even religious these activities might have
seemed while you were alive.

To help you grasp the purpose of our "show and
test" in heaven, picture two followers of Jesus
approaching the bema. One is a high-ranking church
leader, the other a street vendor. First one and then the
other stands for judgment. Each in turn sees every
work he did piled high on the altar. Then the pile is
tested by fire.

Who of these two will step into eternity with the
most reward?

The fire will make the truth obvious to all.

The answer is that before the fire of the bema, *we can't possibly know*. Until then, only God knows what any person's work for Him is worth. That's why Paul encouraged Christians to "judge nothing before the time, until the Lord comes.... Then each one's praise will come from God" (1 Corinthians 4:5).

Only after the test by fire will we finally see how a person's life has added up for eternity. The fire will make the truth obvious to all. And when we see it, we will completely agree with the judgment of Jesus and the reward or loss that follows.

THE GOLD STANDARD

By now you might be wondering what would cause a work to either burn like straw or endure like gold. Obviously the fire would need to test not only *what* we did, but also *how* and *why* we did it.

In the previous chapter, we painted a portrait to show what a life God rewards might look like. But Jesus said that genuine good behavior always begins in the heart (Luke 6:43–45).

Think of the three tests that follow—all gleaned from the teachings of Jesus—as the gold standard to help you evaluate whether the work you do for God will endure:

1. *The Test of Relationship.* It might relieve you to know that a life God rewards is not about performance apart from relationship with Jesus. In fact, just the opposite is true. Jesus said unless His followers stay close to Him and obey His commands, they will not bear "much fruit" for Him—"for without Me you can do nothing" (John 15:5).

   In the book of Revelation, Jesus commended the church at Ephesus for its many good works, but was grieved because they had not kept their love for Him alive. He said, "I know your works, your labor, your patience…. Nevertheless I have this against you, that you have left your first love" (2:2, 4).

2. *The Test of Motive.* Jesus said, "Take heed that you do not do your charitable deeds before men, to be seen by them. Otherwise you have no reward from

your Father in heaven" (Matthew 6:1). What should be our motive? To serve God and bring Him glory. Even ordinary actions like eating and drinking can bring God glory (1 Corinthians 10:31). By contrast, our most "religious" action is worthless if our motive is to build up our own egos or reputations.

3. *The Test of Love.* True good works are always focused on sincerely trying to improve the well-being of another. Jesus said, "But love your enemies, do good, and lend, hoping for nothing in return; and your reward will be great, and you will be sons of the Most High. For He is kind to the unthankful and evil" (Luke 6:35). In Paul's famous passage on love, he pointed out that without love, good deeds will not benefit the doer: "Though I bestow all my goods to feed the poor, and though I give my body to be burned, but have not love, it profits me nothing" (1 Corinthians 13:3).

While it's important to remember that everything we do for God will be judged at the bema, we don't have to be anxious that a work will fail the test of the bema because of something we never heard about.

Jesus will bring no criterion to the judgment that He hasn't clearly revealed in Scripture and empowered us to meet by His Spirit (2 Peter 1:2–4).

So what did Paul mean by the words *suffer loss?*

"How Could I 'Lose' in Heaven?"

The tested-by-fire passage in 1 Corinthians 3 ends with a very sobering prospect: "If anyone's work is burned, he will *suffer loss;* but he himself will be saved, yet so as through fire" (v. 15).

This is the part about our futures that so few believers I know have ever grasped: When we stand before the bema of Jesus, *we may suffer loss.*

What a startling thought! Is it possible that a true follower of Jesus—even though his or her salvation is not at risk at the bema—could step into eternity with few good works to show for his or her lifetime on earth?

Yes. That is exactly what could happen, according to these passages.

It seems clear from these passages that you could do a work and then lose the reward for it. No wonder the apostle John warned, "Look to yourselves, that we do not lose those things we worked for, but that we may receive a full reward" (2 John 1:8).

No wonder he pleaded, "Little children, abide in Him, that when He appears, we may have confidence and not be ashamed before Him at His coming" (1 John 2:28).

Still, the primary purpose of the bema is not loss, but gain. Even though the consequences of missed opportunities and lost reward will go with us into eternity, any regret or shame we might experience will not. How can I be sure? Because the Bible promises that "God will wipe away every tear from their eyes" (Revelation 21:4).

The amazing truth is that, regardless of what happens at the bema, Jesus will not love you any less or any more for all eternity than He loved you when He purchased your life with His own blood—or than He loves you right now as you're reading this book.

Let me leave you with one more surprise: Jesus wants you to keep it all.

Friend, join me in living wholeheartedly for a day of celebration, not disappointment, at the bema. No reward on earth will compare to the pleasure of seeing unclouded joy on the face of our Savior as He reviews the work of our lives, then leans forward to favor us with the reward He most wants to give.

A REWARD TO KEEP

At that moment, when Jesus gives us the reward for our life, when we finally and completely see and understand all that God has done for us and in us and through us—and we know fully that without Him we could not have done even one commendable work for Him—our overwhelming response will be to cry out in thanks and praise to Him.

At that moment, out of sheer joy and gratitude, you'll want to fall in worship at the feet of the Lord Jesus Christ and give back everything He has just given to you. But let me leave you with one more surprise.

Jesus wants you to keep it all.

As we'll see in the next chapter, His plan is for you to enjoy and make good use of your rewards for the rest of eternity. The popular assumption that we will cast our crowns before Christ is based on a well-intentioned misreading of Revelation 4:10–11. There we see a specific group of elders worshiping God by casting their crowns at His feet. Yet the context shows that these elders do not represent all believers. And the verses show that their act of worship—casting their crowns—is repeated over and over throughout eternity.

Will you, like those awestruck worshipers, want to respond unreservedly to God once you see His amazing power and love? Absolutely!

But the *misthos* and *apodidomai* of Jesus are not momentary but *eternal* rewards—the everlasting consequence of your choice to serve Him during your brief time on earth, and the everlasting proof of His limitless love. One of the most dramatic pictures of rewards that last forever is seen in Daniel 12:3: "Those who are wise shall shine like the brightness of the firmament, and those who turn many to righteousness like the stars forever and ever."

And your rewards are meant to be yours eternally.

If you're thinking that as wonderful as they might be, you can't imagine needing or wanting more reward than heaven itself, you're in for a surprise! In the next two chapters, I'll show you from the words of Jesus that the rewards you receive in heaven will determine a lot about what you actually *do* there.

And what you will most want to do in heaven may be the greatest surprise of all.

5

THE QUESTION
OF YOUR LIFE

"Whoever desires to become great among you shall be your

servant.... For even the Son of Man did not come to be

served, but to serve, and to give His life a ransom for many."

JESUS, IN MARK 10:43, 45

Whyou get there, what do you think your most powerful desire in heaven will be?

It took eighty thousand men to give me a clue.

I was part of a capacity crowd of Christian men gathered in Detroit's cavernous Silverdome stadium. When the speaker finished, the worship team stepped up to lead us in the hymn "Holy, Holy, Holy."

What started as a quiet refrain increased in volume with each verse. When we finished the hymn we started over, this time louder. Eventually the stadium seemed to shake—from the playing field to the highest tier—with the sound of our worship.

> *Holy, holy, holy! Lord God Almighty!*
> *Early in the morning our song shall rise to Thee;*
> *Holy, holy, holy!*

We sang it on our knees. We sang it with our arms stretched high. We sang it with our heads thrown back and at the top of our lungs. The worship went on and on until we lost all sense of time and our fingertips seemed to touch the edge of heaven. Just when I thought the volume would blow the stadium roof off, the arena erupted in thunderous applause to God.

I thought that beautiful roar sounded a lot like heaven.

Never had I reached so deep into my soul to worship the Lord. Yet the deeper my expression of worship became, the more desperate I felt to do something more. At one point I turned and shouted to a friend, "I want to worship more deeply,

We will

desperately

long to do

something more.

but I can't find any place to go!"

Years later, the sound of those men's voices united in praise still echoes in my memory. I remember, too, what I felt in my own heart that day. And I can imagine when I'm worshiping in the very presence of God with an innumerable host, I'll feel it a hundred times more. That's why I think in heaven I'll feel something close to...*desperation.*

Does that word surprise you?

When you and I stand together in the presence of God—knowing and seeing who He is and all that He has done in His sovereign power to move us from birth to "that Day"—we will pour out our thanks and praise to Him, joyfully doing our best to shake the rafters of heaven.

But I'm also convinced that we will desperately long to do something more.

That's what this chapter is about.

WHAT YOU WILL CRAVE

The words and example of Jesus, along with my experience in the Silverdome, convince me that *in heaven we will desperately crave to serve.*

When we see our Savior, we will be swept up in a

consuming, eternity-long desire to respond in love to Jesus—and worship and praise won't be enough. We will want to *do* something for Him.

Think about it: When you and I love someone with all our heart, words are wonderful and precious, but we're compelled to go beyond words to action. We long to give, to help, to protect, to serve.

Words weren't enough for God, either.

Words weren't enough for God, either. He loved every person in His world so much that He did something dramatic: He gave His Son in order to save us (John 3:16). And Jesus said that the greatest expression of love is to do something—"to lay down one's life for his friends" (John 15:13).

In this chapter we'll see the direct connection between how well we manage our life for God on earth and how much our Lord will graciously allow us to serve Him in heaven.

THE QUESTION OF YOUR LIFE

Again and again, Jesus told stories about servants commissioned to take care of a valuable asset that belonged to the master (for example, money, fields, or vineyards). A helpful word to describe this role and one the Bible uses is *steward*.

What distinguishes a steward from a servant? Both a steward and a servant serve someone, both have a responsibility, and both work for a wage. The difference is that a steward has been charged with managing his master's assets. In Jesus' stories, we often see a pattern: The servant/steward is charged with managing something important for his master while the master is away for an extended period.

Picture the key events of a steward's service in a timeline:

Begin .... *End*

The Commission of the Steward	The Master Leaves	The Opportunity of the Steward	The Master Returns	The Reward of the Steward

You can easily identify the one step where the steward has the chance to either fail or succeed at his mission and impact his future—it is his "opportunity."

Jesus told parables about stewards for an important and specific reason: He would soon be going away. During His absence, the business of His kingdom on earth would be delegated to His followers. They would be commissioned to spend their lives greatly increasing His kingdom. In the future He would return, ask for an accounting, and reward His servants "each according to his works" (Matthew 16:27).

If you are a Christian, you are in the same circumstance as the early followers of Jesus.

You have been commissioned to manage an asset for your Master. Your asset is your life—the sum of your talents, strengths, personality, and interests. Your opportunity is to manage your life in such a way that you greatly increase your Master's kingdom. Your Master has not yet returned, and every day you should answer this question:

How will I steward what my Master has placed in my care?

*The stewards'
assignment?
"Do business till
I come."*

In fact, every day you *are* answering this question. In the parables we're about to look at, this truth is quietly but plainly evident. Whether you act intentionally on your commission or not, you are deciding by your actions and attitudes how you will steward your opportunity for God.

Since our Master is not physically present, good stewardship always requires faith—faith that our Master is who He said He is, faith that what He asked us to do matters now and will matter when He returns, and faith that He *will* return.

No wonder the Bible uses the word *faithful* more than any other to describe the conduct of a good steward. Paul said that the one nearly defined the other: "It is required in stewards that one be found faithful" (1 Corinthians 4:2).

"DO BUSINESS TILL I COME"

Jesus' two best-known parables about stewardship, the Parable of the Minas and the Parable of the Talents, both start with ordinary people in ordinary situations but quickly enter into surprising territory.

In the Parable of the Minas, found in Luke 19, a nobleman must leave town. He calls ten servants and gives each one a mina (about three years' wages). The stewards' assignment? "Do business till I come" (v. 13).

When the nobleman returns, he calls for an accounting. The first servant reports a tenfold increase on his investment of his master's mina. The master responds, "Well done, good servant; because you were faithful in a very little, have authority over ten cities" (v. 17).

The second servant reports a fivefold return, and the master gives him an exactly proportionate reward: "You also be over five cities" (v. 19). Yet what is most notable is what the master *doesn't* say to him—he doesn't say, "Well done," or "good servant," or even "because you were faithful in a very little." The lesser level of commendation shows that the Master knew the servant could have done more to multiply his mina.

The third steward simply returns the mina he was given, explaining that he kept the money safely hidden at home.

Imagine his shame when his master calls him a "wicked servant" (v. 22), then takes his one mina and gives it to the servant who already had ten! The nobleman explains his action with a startling statement: "To everyone who has will be given; and from him who does not have, even what he has will be taken away from him" (v. 26).

Does the nobleman's response seem fair to you?

When I teach on this parable, audiences often rush to defend the third servant. "Wasn't he just being careful?" they say. "Besides, he didn't *lose* anything." Yet it doesn't take long, as we talk about how we make decisions as parents, managers, or owners, for us to agree: We invariably give the greatest future opportunity to the person who has proven to be the most productive with the present opportunity.

Audiences often rush to defend the third servant.

Fortunately for us, Jesus' parable shows the responses of all three stewards—and we can discover life-changing insights from each.

GREAT EXPECTATIONS

Let's look at three common misbeliefs about steward-ship among Christians today and the corresponding truth Jesus wants us to see:

- We think that even though God gave us our gifts and talents, He is not bothered if we don't make the most of every opportunity.

But the *Truth of the First Steward* shows us that God expects us to take the resources of our lives and *greatly multiply* them for His kingdom.

- We think that if God does reward us for serving Him, His reward will be a general commendation that will apply to everyone equally and won't change our future opportunities in His kingdom.

But the *Truth of the Second Steward* is that God will reward our work for Him, but it will be in direct *proportion* to how much we have multiplied our life for Him. His response will have a major and eternal impact on our future.

- We think that if we don't serve God with what He's given us, the worst that could happen would be no reward.

But the *Truth of the Third Steward* is that if we do not use what God has placed in our care for Him, we will *suffer loss*—of both the potential reward we could have earned, and the opportunity to serve God more fully in eternity.

TEN-MINA MAN

I remember when the radical implications of these truths exploded into my mind and heart. Although I was very familiar with the parable, I'd never asked myself: *Am I a ten-mina steward?*

The question launched a season of sober reevaluation and radical change in my life. Finally, a breakthrough came. I chose to believe that since a ten-mina life was God's purpose for me, I would take it as the best measure of stewardship in my life. I committed to God that by His grace I would become a ten-mina man for Him.

But maybe by now you're thinking, *I don't have*

many talents or opportunities, so how can I bring God much return for my life? And does that mean I won't have the chance to serve Him much in eternity?

An encouraging answer from Jesus is found in the Parable of the Talents (Matthew 25:14–30). The story follows the same pattern as the Parable of the Minas. But this time, three stewards are each given *different amounts* of money—"to each according to his own ability" (v. 15).

In this case, two servants double what they have been given. Yet when the master returns, he gives the *same commendation and reward* to both. Why? Because a servant's reward is based on total results *in light of potential*. The master tells both servants the same thing:

> "Well done, good and faithful servant; you were faithful over a few things, I will make you ruler over many things. Enter into the joy of your lord."
>
> VV. 21, 23

In the same way, Jesus will reward you and me on the basis of what each of us did with what we were given.

Are you a seamstress or the leader of a nation? A factory worker or a young mother? A village pastor or a builder? Every disciple has the same opportunity for productivity now, and the same opportunity for great reward later. In fact, your future is as promising and important as the future of the most gifted person in history.

For Sheila, a mother of toddlers, ten-mina living has meant turning sincere intentions into a sensible plan—a weekly friendship group for struggling young moms in her neighborhood.

For Mark, a developer in Arizona, ten-mina living has meant redefining what "do business" implies. Increasingly, he is rearranging his workload so he can spend the majority of his time providing building services at no cost to mission projects in Central America.

For Jennifer, who went blind at the age of fifteen, ten-mina living has meant that boundary lines have become starting lines. She now calls her blindness "my difficult gift" and is reaching thousands through music and speaking.

I hope you never again think of faithfully serving God as merely not sinning a lot, doing "business as usual," or just not quitting. True faithfulness as a steward is much closer to *extraordinary entrepreneurial excellence!*

THE STEWARD'S REWARD

I opened this chapter telling you why I believed we will desperately want to serve God in heaven. *Doing* is a servant's language of devotion. In heaven, more opportunity to do God's will through loving service will be our highest reward.

Exactly how *much* opportunity will faithful stewards receive in heaven? So much that in the upside-down kingdom of heaven, the highest word for serving is *ruling*. We can trace this surprising reversal to the Garden of Eden. Remember that at Creation God made both woman and man for a particular task—to serve Him on earth by steward-ing His creation. Jesus con-firmed this purpose when He told His disciples that their reward in heaven for serving Him here would be to sit on twelve thrones and judge the tribes of Israel (Matthew 19:28).

Doing is a servant's language of devotion.

Ruling in heaven will have *nothing* in common with the corruption and manipulation we're so used to seeing in displays of power on earth! When the curse of sin is removed and you and I are restored to our creation purpose, we will be free to rule for God to our fullest powers while bringing only the highest good to ourselves and to others.

Your commission for Jesus is as big as the world.

Ruling is also the reward for serving we see in Jesus' parables of faithful stewards. Did you notice? In the mina parable, the highest reward for service was to "have authority over ten cities" (Luke 19:17). And in the Parable of the Talents, the reward is similar—"I will make you ruler over many things" (Matthew 25:21, 23).

Serve faithfully here, rule perfectly there.

My friend, I challenge you to see your true calling today and to seize the opportunity that is right in front of you. Don't waste another day living for less. Your commission for Jesus is as big as the world

(Mark 16:15). Your opportunity is now. Serve Him faithfully on earth and you will be wonderfully, fully, perfectly prepared to do what you will desperately crave to do in heaven.

And on that Day, you will hear Jesus tell you from His heart, "Well done, good and faithful servant…enter into the joy of your Lord."

6

THE GOD WHO
GIVES BACK

"Do not lay up for yourselves treasures on earth, where moth and rust destroy and where thieves break in and steal; but lay up for yourselves treasures in heaven, where neither moth nor rust destroys and where thieves do not break in and steal."

JESUS, IN MATTHEW 6:19–20

I was taking a coffee break during a family conference in Kentucky when Will walked up and stood beside my chair. He was about nine. He asked if I wanted to donate to a missions project.

"What would you use my money for?" I asked.

Will held out a radio. "This radio runs by sun power," he said proudly. "It's for people who live in the jungles. People can listen to this radio to learn things and hear about Jesus."

I decided on the spot to make Will an offer. "Tell

you what," I said, "I'll give to your project, but I have a rule that says you have to give money first." On one of his donation cards, I wrote out my proposal:

Will,
If you give one to five dollars,
     I'll give double what you give.
If you give six to ten dollars,
     I'll give triple what you give.
If you give eleven to twenty dollars,
     I'll give four times what you give.

I signed my name and Will read the card. By the time he was finished, his eyes were as big as saucers. Then suddenly his face fell, and he stared at the floor.

"Don't you like my idea?" I asked.

"Yeah," he said, shuffling his feet.

"Well, what are you going to do?"

"Nothing."

"Nothing?"

"I can't," he said. "I already gave everything I had."

I felt a pang in my heart. "You mean you put all your money in your own fund drive?" I asked.

He nodded.

"So you can't buy any more snacks for the rest of the conference?"

He nodded again.

At that moment, I knew what I needed to do. "Actually, Will," I began, "I also have a rule that if you give everything you have, I will give everything I have, too."

As it happened, I'd just been to a bank to withdraw a considerable amount of cash for my trip. I reached under the table for my briefcase, pulled out a bank envelope of bills, and handed it to Will.

I'm not sure who was more surprised—Will or me. Now both of us had eyes as big as saucers, but we were both grinning happily.

My experience with Will has come to illustrate a truth for me about giving that's so surprising it hardly sounds possible: *Whatever I give to God on earth He will more than give back to me in heaven.*

In this chapter we will explore what Jesus said about how to make our money and possessions count in eternity.

A GENEROUS MATCHING PLAN

What did Jesus really teach about money and possessions?

Peter may have first heard it clearly when he listened to Jesus telling a wealthy young man why he should leave his possessions and money to follow Him: "You will have treasure in heaven" (Matthew 19:21).

When the man turned down Jesus' offer and left, Peter stepped forward to ask the obvious question:

> *"See, we have left all and followed You. Therefore what shall we have?"*
>
> V. 27

I love the fact that Jesus didn't scold Peter for his self-interest. Or smile and say, "I wasn't actually *serious* about treasure in heaven." Instead, He gave a most revealing answer. Jesus told Peter that he and the other disciples would rule over the nation of Israel when He set up His kingdom. Then He said that every person who leaves all to follow Him would be repaid a hundredfold (Matthew 19:29).

A hundredfold is the equivalent of a 10,000 percent return!

Now you can see that what happened to nine-year-old Will only hints at God's amazing plan to reward every believer who sacrifices treasure on earth to serve Him. Suddenly my "generous" matching of Will's donation appears meager next to God's extravagant promise.

WHAT JESUS SAID YOU SHOULD DO WITH TREASURE

Perhaps Jesus' most familiar teaching on treasure is found in the Sermon on the Mount:

> *"Do not lay up for yourselves treasures on earth, where moth and rust destroy and where thieves break in and steal; but lay up for yourselves treasures in heaven."*

MATTHEW 6:19–20

If you grew up in church like I did, you may assume that these verses mean spiritual pursuits are more important than earthly ones. But Jesus was

clearly talking about actual
treasure and how you can keep
it. He used the same word to
describe real treasure on earth
and real treasure in heaven
(translated *thesauros* in Greek).
He didn't reveal what treasure in
heaven would look like or how
it would be measured, but it *will*
be highly valuable.

*Jesus shatters
three common
misconceptions about
how we should think
about treasure.*

Suppose your accountant
said to you: "If you invest your
treasure in Bank A, you will lose it. But if you invest
your treasure in Bank B, you will save it."

You'd never assume that while your accountant
referred to your hard-earned money when she men-
tioned Bank A, she meant only your spiritual treasures
when she recommended Bank B! Why, then, should
we think that eternal treasure will be anything less
than real and highly desirable?

Here, in just one verse (Matthew 6:20), Jesus shatters three common misconceptions about how we
should think about treasure:

1. *What you should do with your treasure—"lay up."* The Greek verb, translated "lay up," is in the imperative in this verse—it's Jesus' command. He wants you to know that laying up treasure is God's plan for you and is a directive you should obey.

2. *Who you should lay it up for—"yourselves."* Each of us must lay up treasure individually. Jesus reveals that if you don't lay up treasure for yourself in heaven, no one can do it for you. That's why Jesus called the man who never laid up treasure for himself a "fool" (Luke 12:13–21). Jesus never rewards selfishness, only *selflessness*. As you're going to see, to lay up treasure for ourselves in heaven, we must first give it to others on earth.

3. *Where you should lay it up—"in heaven."* Location matters. If you lay up treasure on earth, as Jesus pointed out, it's vulnerable to corruption or loss. The truth is that heaven is the only place where your treasure will be safe.

By now you might be asking, "But why would treasure matter to me in heaven?"

I understand the question. Yet we have to conclude from Jesus' dramatic statements here and elsewhere that our treasure will matter greatly to us in eternity!

In God's kingdom, when the sinful pull of greed, envy, and manipulation is absent, we will *enjoy* our treasure, and it will serve a pure and meaningful purpose. As we'll see, our treasure will allow us to serve, to give, to accomplish, and to enjoy more for Him.

But there's something very specific we must do, Jesus said, to "transfer" our treasure to heaven.

Getting It from Here to There

I remember years ago, when Darlene Marie and I moved across the country. As we stood in our driveway watching the moving truck pull away, it occurred to me that aside from the bare essentials, the truck contained our most important belongings and personal treasures. Since our plan was to follow later by car, we wouldn't see our possessions again until weeks later, when we arrived at our new home.

We forward the treasure of our lives on to heaven a lot like that. We stay behind with the essentials. But the real goods—if we intend to keep their value through eternity—must go on ahead.

Think of it as God's moving plan: *To move your treasure to heaven, you have to send it ahead.*

How do we accomplish that? One day, Jesus explained His moving plan to His disciples:

"Sell what you have and give alms; provide your-selves money bags which do not grow old, a trea-sure in the heavens that does not fail, where no thief approaches nor moth destroys."

LUKE 12:33

This verse clearly shows the link between an action regarding treasure on earth and the result of that action in heaven. If you "give alms" now, Jesus told His friends, you will actually "provide [for] yourselves" something valuable later—"a treasure in the heavens."

I hope it's evident to you that Jesus wasn't telling His disciples that treasure doesn't matter, or that He didn't want them to have any. Just the opposite! He wanted them to provide for themselves *because* He knew that treasure will matter in eternity, and He wanted them to have a lot of it there.

Paul told Timothy to command the well-to-do members of his church to "be rich in good works, ready to give, willing to share, *storing up for themselves a good foundation for the time to come"* (1 Timothy 6:18–19).

Notice the pattern of teaching: Followers of Jesus are to store up "for themselves," and the reason lies in the unbreakable link—their action affects "the time to come."

Do you want to store up "treasure in the heavens that does not fail"? Then surrender it to God's priorities here. That is the only way.

EVERYTHING YOU OWN IS ON LOAN

Just as you'd expect, the principles of stewardship (responsibility, faithfulness, growth, and potential) apply to our treasure.

In one of His teachings about money and possessions in heaven, Jesus said:

> *"He who is faithful in what is least is faithful also in much.... Therefore if you have not been faithful in the unrighteous mammon, who will commit to your trust the true riches? And if you have not been faithful in what is another man's, who will give you what is your own?"*

> LUKE 16:10–12

Here, Jesus is describing how a steward can succeed with someone else's money. Not surprisingly, He
uses the word *faithful* four times!

What *is* surprising is what Jesus promises a faithful steward of treasure. It is not, as you might expect,
that you will steward more treasure in heaven, but that
you will *own* it. Instead of having the "unrighteous
mammon" of earth, you will have the "true riches" of
heaven; instead of managing "what is another man's,"
you will have "what is your own."

In other words, if you do well with what you *think*
is your own now, you'll get what is *really* your own later.

THE SUM OF YOUR OPPORTUNITIES

You can probably look around your circle of acquain-
tances and find your own favorite examples of giving
away earthly treasure. Here are a few of mine:

- Marcellus gave away his entire wardrobe to
  homeless men (and Marcellus is a man of excep-
  tional taste in clothing).
- Ira and Francis cashed in a retirement fund so
  they could support themselves while they volunteered full-time at a drug treatment program.

- Seven men shaved off all their hair to show support for a dying friend who had lost his hair because of cancer treatments.
- Mariba gave her most cherished painting to a discouraged friend.
- Nathan and Anna sold their large home and downsized so they could free up substantial funds for God's work.

No matter how large or small your gift, you put your life in motion by answering two simple questions:

1. *"What treasure has God given me?"* The same principle of potential we saw in the last chapter also applies to stewarding treasure. God evaluates faithfulness based on our potential—how much we give of what He has entrusted us with. Jesus commended the widow for giving her pennies because proportionately she was giving far more than the rich (Luke 21:4).

2. *"What is God asking me to do with my treasure?"* After giving to the church, ask God for guidance about where to give beyond that. One investment is not as good as another. Ask yourself what God cares

about most. For example, will directing your giving to a high-profile civic fund please Him as much as giving it to your church's missions fund?

The solution is simple, probably difficult, and absolutely life changing.

The people I've met who are most faithful with their money are also the most free of its entanglements. They are the ones I admire most, because they understand that if you don't serve God with your money, you will serve your money.

A RIVAL MASTER

The treasure God asks you to serve Him with is the very force in your life that threatens your loyalties to your Master. Jesus said:

> *"No servant can serve two masters; for either he will hate the one and love the other, or else he will be loyal to the one and despise the other. You cannot serve God and mammon."*

LUKE 16:13

When you serve God, you are using God's money to accomplish His wishes. But when you serve money, you are using God's money to accomplish your wishes. And when you do that, you will inevitably follow your human instincts to keep your money *here*.

But Jesus said, "Where your treasure is, there your heart will be also" (Matthew 6:21).

So let me ask you, where is your heart right now? If you aren't purposefully and generously investing your treasure in God's kingdom, I promise you it's because your heart isn't there.

The solution is simple, probably difficult, and absolutely life changing. Don't wait for your heart to move on its own, my friend, because it might never happen. Instead, apply what you've learned from the words of Jesus. Begin to move your treasure today to what matters in heaven…and your heart will follow.

7

THE FIRST KEY

"For God did not send His Son into

the world to condemn the world,

but that the world through Him might be saved."

JESUS, IN JOHN 3:17

Rudy had that look. His wife had just intro-
duced him to me at the front of the church,
then "unexpectedly" left to attend to other
matters. Rudy stood there awkwardly, hands shoved in
his pockets. I'm sure he would have given half his life
savings to be delivered from my presence.

I smiled and asked how I could help.

"My wife wants me to get religion," he said, scuffing
the carpet with the toe of his shoe.

I asked him why.

He grimaced. "So I don't go to hell."

"Are you planning to go to hell sometime soon?" I asked.

He looked at me, then burst out laughing. He seemed relieved to find that a Bible teacher might have a sense of humor.

"So," I continued, "when you stand before God, what's going to keep you out of hell?"

Dead silence, then Rudy chuckled. "I guess I never thought about it quite like that."

He continued hesitantly, "I'm not a bad person, you know. I don't run around on my wife like some of my friends. And I try to be a nice guy most of the time...."

A smile crossed his face. He liked how my answer was shaping up.

I decided to help him out. "So God probably has a big scale, wouldn't you think? On one side would be your sins—you do sin, don't you, Rudy?"

He nodded.

I continued. "And on the other would be all those

91

good things you do for your wife, your kids, your community, and so on. Am I on the right track?"

Rudy nodded with more enthusiasm.

"And when God puts your life on His big scale, you'll have more good than bad, and everything will be okay, right?"

A smile crossed his face. He liked how my answer was shaping up. I told him that it all made sense to me, too, but I had a question. I took out my pen and drew a line like this:

TOTALLY EVIL ————————— TOTALLY GOOD
(0 percent good)   *(100 percent good)*

"Clearly," I said, "you just need to decide how much more good than bad you need for the scale to tilt in your favor." I handed Rudy my pen and asked him to put an *x* on the line to mark how close to "Totally Good" he'd have to get to be good enough for heaven.

Rudy studied my pad, then started to mark an *x* at about 60 percent. Then he reconsidered and moved it closer to 75 percent, then paused to think again. Finally he shook his head and drew a rather feeble *x* at about the 70 percent spot.

He handed me back my pen without looking up.

I pointed to his mark. "Let's say you hit your spot right on the nose, Rudy, because you really aren't that bad of a guy. But what if when you meet your Maker He reveals to you that, unfortunately, the x spot is farther to the right—say at 71 percent. If you were 70 percent 'good' but God said the minimum required was actually 71 percent, where would a person like you go?"

He crossed his arms, still not looking at me. "Hell, I guess."

"Then finding out where the actual x is on that line would be the most important question of your life, right?" I asked.

That was the day my new friend hit God's mark perfectly.

Rudy grunted in agreement. "Yeah, I'm just not too sure where it ought to be."

I closed my notepad and started picking up my things, but Rudy wasn't moving. "Can I know exactly where the x is?" he asked. "Cause I really need to know. Maybe you could take another minute and show me?"

I was hoping he would feel that way. We found a seat in a quiet corner, and I showed him what the Bible says about that *x*. He understood, he responded...and that was the day my new friend hit God's mark perfectly.

The Name of the Problem

The first six chapters of the book focused on the second key to your eternity—how your works affect your repayment in heaven. It's time to talk about the first key. As you may recall, the first key is *belief*—what you believe determines where you will spend your forever.

In a book where there has been so much talk about what you need to *do* to get the most out of your life, you're going to love what you learn about the key of belief. The teachings of Jesus show us that our belief works where our works don't—and for a very important reason.

Someone has already done the work for you!

Someone or something had put it in Rudy's mind that if he wanted to gain entrance to heaven, he had a problem that only good works could fix. Millions of thoughtful people around the world think the same way. But according to Jesus, Rudy and all those millions of others are trying to solve the right problem with the wrong key.

Let me show you what I mean.

Notice that it never entered Rudy's mind that his standing with God was secure—because he knew it wasn't. He had a problem, and it's that very problem that he was trying to fix with his good works. The name for this problem is sin. Everyone knows by experience that they have sinned repeatedly.

Paul wrote that it is God who plants this awareness in us:

> *For the wrath of God is revealed from heaven against all ungodliness and unrighteousness of men, who suppress the truth in unrighteousness, because what may be known of God is manifest in them, for God has shown it to them.*
>
> ROMANS 1:18–19

And because God also reveals His existence and His attributes to us, said Paul, this awareness of our sin problem leaves us without excuse:

> *For since the creation of the world His invisible attributes are clearly seen, being understood by the things that are made, even His eternal power and Godhead, so that they are without excuse, because, although they knew God, they did not glorify Him as God.*

VV. 20–21

These verses sum up the very real human problem that every major religion in the world is trying to solve: *Since we know that we deserve God's judgment, what can we do to make things right with Him and escape the consequences of our sin?*

Some religions seek to appease the spirit world through activities such as animal sacrifices or paying money to a witch doctor or shaman. Some religions teach that people can atone for sin by enduring suffering now—for example, crawling for miles on their knees, or beating themselves—so they won't suffer later. Other religions teach that people can make up for their wrongs by doing more right. That was Rudy's religion.

But none of these religious approaches can solve the universal problem of sin. Why? Because they rely on our good works, and as we'll see in a minute, the consequences of our sin are so severe that no amount of good works on our part can rescue us.

Jesus taught that your works for God on earth can greatly benefit you in eternity once your sin problem has been resolved and heaven is your destination. But this raises a sobering question: What value, if any, could good works have in eternity if you haven't yet resolved your sin problem and hell is your destination?

No amount of good works on our part can rescue us.

Jesus showed that although good works are useless to get anyone into heaven, *they still matter.*

HELL BY DEGREES

Has it ever bothered you to think that your scrupulously moral and kind neighbor who does not believe in Jesus will suffer to the same degree as Hitler in eternity? Something deep in your spirit says that wouldn't be fair.

That's because it wouldn't be.

If the unbreakable link—which says that actions on earth have consequences in eternity—applies equally to every person, it should apply whether your destination is heaven or hell.

In fact, since Jesus reveals that there will be degrees of reward in heaven, wouldn't it make sense that a just God would judge nonbelievers in the same way—with degrees of retribution?

It's time to tell you what I told Rudy.

That's exactly what Jesus said. Specifically, He revealed that suffering in hell has the potential to increase according to how a person lived his life. We see this truth first in Jesus' condemnation:

"And you, Capernaum...will be brought down to Hades; for if the mighty works which were done in you had been done in Sodom, it would have remained until this day. But I say to you that it shall be more tolerable for the land of Sodom in the day of judgment than for you."

MATTHEW 11:23–24

98

Notice the phrase *more tolerable*. The word *more* in that phrase indicates that different degrees of tolerability and judgment exist in hell.

On another occasion, Jesus told the Pharisees that they would "receive greater condemnation" for using their position to prey on widows and for making long prayers for pretense (Matthew 23:14). The apostle Paul wrote that some were "treasuring up for [themselves] wrath in the day of wrath" (Romans 2:5). The apostle John said that unbelievers would be judged, "each one according to [in proportion to] his works" (Revelation 20:13).

But don't be confused: Your good works can never lessen the torment of hell, in the same way that an evil work (sin) can't lessen the joys of heaven. Here's a helpful way to remember the truth of degrees of compensation:

> *Heaven never gets worse, only better;*
> *hell never gets better, only worse.*

Isn't it time for you to pick up on the only key that will unlock heaven for you? Now it's time to tell you what I told Rudy.

WHY WORKS WON'T WORK

Rudy was ready to learn where the x should go. I pointed to the "100 percent good" mark and said, "The Bible says that's where the x has to be."

"But that's impossible!" Rudy replied. "Then no one would go to heaven."

"So you agree that no one can be 100 percent good and solve the problem of sin on his own?"

"Yes, I guess so."

"And what if I told you that the penalty for sin—for even one sin—is death?"

"Well, that wouldn't seem fair at all," he said. "No one's perfect. Everyone sins—but the punishment is still death?"

"Well, that wouldn't seem fair at all," he said. "No one's perfect."

I reassured Rudy that he was thinking logically. Then I opened my Bible and showed him that ever since Adam and Eve sinned in the Garden, death—both physical and spiritual—has been the consequence. In Genesis we read, "For in the day that you eat of it you shall surely die" (Genesis 2:17). And in the New Testament, Rudy saw that the problem is still with us: "For the wages of sin is *death*" (Romans 6:23).

"Think of it this way," I continued. "Let's say I went before a judge and was sentenced to die. But I told the judge, 'Please, sir, let me live, and I promise I'll do a lot of community service.' Would that work?"

"Of course not!" said Rudy. After a minute he said, "So there's no solution, is there? There's no hope."

"Exactly," I said. "There's no hope—" I paused for a moment before continuing—"unless you could find a substitute. What if someone volunteered to substitute for you—to stand in your place—when it came time for God to judge you?"

"That would be great," he said. "But you said they'd have to be 100 percent good, and no one is, right?"

"Exactly—no one except Jesus." I went on to explain to Rudy that the Bible says Jesus was God's Son and He alone lived on this earth without sin. In fact, God sent His Son to earth so that He could be Rudy's substitute, die in Rudy's place, and pay the penalty for his sin—and the whole world's sin—once and for all.

Then I pulled out my notebook again. I pointed to

the *x* Rudy had drawn. "You have a choice to make, Rudy."

"Okay," he said.

I pointed at his *x*. "You can believe in your good works—and hope you're right about the *x*. Or you can believe in Jesus Christ and His death on your behalf."

I urge you to believe that what Jesus said is true.

"Definitely the second choice," he said. "It makes way more sense."

I opened my Bible and read to Rudy how Jesus explained the choice that lay before him.

"For God so loved the world that He gave His only begotten Son, that whoever believes in Him should not perish but have everlasting life. For God did not send His Son into the world to condemn the world, but that the world through Him might be saved."

JOHN 3:16–17

Friend, maybe it's the choice before you, too.

If you have been reading this chapter and you're

not sure that heaven is your destination, I urge you to put your faith in what Jesus said. If you want to put your full trust in Him, then why not pray the same prayer Rudy did:

> *Dear God, I am sorry for my sins, and now I know I can't do anything to fix them. So I accept Your Son's death as full payment for my sins, and I receive the Lord Jesus Christ as my Savior. And Jesus, I'm going to start serving You right now! In Your name, amen.*

This is a prayer God always answers and is delighted to hear.

DESTINATION HEAVEN

If you just put your full trust in Jesus for your salvation, your eternal destination has already permanently changed—from hell to heaven!

Now you are a new creation in Jesus (2 Corinthians 5:17). Now you have eternal life (John 3:16–17). Now you are a child of God and an heir of salvation (Galatians 4:7).

And from this moment on, you don't have to hope that your good works will add up to your salvation, because like every other true follower of Jesus, you now understand the meaning of these well-known verses:

> *By grace you have been saved through faith, and that not of yourselves; it is the gift of God, not of works, lest anyone should boast.*
>
> EPHESIANS 2:8–9

Because of this grace, you will never experience in eternity the negative consequences of your sins—because Jesus took those on Himself.

Instead, you can begin responding with your whole heart of love for God and with service for Him, knowing that He will want to reward you for everything you do for Him.

Look at the very next verse:

> *For we are His workmanship, created in Christ Jesus for good works, which God prepared before-hand that we should walk in them.*
>
> V. 10

You, my friend, have been created and saved to do good works!

And if you just placed your trust in Jesus Christ, then for the first time in your life, you are truly ready to live a life God rewards.

8

SEEING THROUGH
TO FOREVER

"And behold, I am coming quickly, and My reward is with Me, to give to every one according to his work."

JESUS, IN REVELATION 22:12

When your alarm clock goes off tomorrow morning, eternity will be nowhere in sight.

You'll put on your eyeglasses, fumble with your collar. You'll greet your family, have a strong cup of coffee or tea, walk out into your day…and make the first choice of your new life.

Will I live for what I can see, knowing it will soon disappear? Or will I live for eternity?

This book has tried to show you beyond all doubt

what Jesus wanted you to know so you could make the right choice.

Yet no matter how hard you look, you won't find visible proof of your future in heaven. Why? "We do not look at the things which are seen," wrote Paul, "but at the things which are not seen. For the things which are seen are temporary" (2 Corinthians 4:18).

Earth may be temporary, but it sure is convincing, isn't it? Without faith, we could never see or even imagine our true destination.

I'll never forget hearing the story in graduate school of a missionary couple from Great Britain who had spent a lifetime serving God in some far corner of the earth. The century turned. After forty years, they wrote their supporters that they were coming home and sailed for England.

When they laid eyes on their country's coastline for the first time in decades, the man said to his wife, "I wonder if anyone will be here to welcome us home."

As the ship sailed into Plymouth Harbor, the elderly couple stood at the upper deck of the ocean liner, holding hands. Then, to their surprise and pleasure, they saw that throngs of people crowded the

Earth may

be temporary,

but it sure is

convincing, isn't it?

dock, pointing in their direction and cheering. A band played. Men held up a banner that read, "Welcome home! We're proud of you!"

The husband was deeply moved. "Isn't this wonderful!" His wife laughed happily, and they decided it was time to go below to collect their luggage.

But as they emerged onto the gangplank, their hearts pounding with anticipation, they were taken aback. The crowd had already started to disperse. Soon, it became clear what had happened. The huge welcome was not for them, but for a politician returning from some foreign success. In fact, no one was there to greet them at all.

The husband couldn't hide his disappointment. "After a lifetime of service, this isn't much of a welcome home."

His wife took his arm. "Come along, sweetheart," she said softly. "This is just England. We're not home yet."

THE BOOK OF REMEMBRANCE

Doesn't it strike you that a major reason so many followers of Jesus are not wholeheartedly serving God is that we base our expectation of reward on visible proof? We may not often admit it, but we expect an immediate consequence for our good choices; then if we don't see one, *we conclude that there must be no eternal consequence.*

I remember several hundred Christian workers at a retreat in the Midwest who had been temporarily blinded by the immediate. By our second day together, the depth of their discouragement became obvious. I asked, "How many of you would say that even though you love God, right now you feel ready to give up? For what you put into your ministry, it just isn't worth it?"

More than half raised a hand.

Together we opened our Bibles to the last page of the Old Testament. There we met another group of God's servants who wanted to live for God but were seeing no benefit. In fact, they had concluded based on what they could see that those who didn't give God's will a second thought seemed more blessed than they (Malachi 3:15). Here is what they said:

"It is useless to serve God;
What profit is it that we have kept His ordinance?"

v. 14

Do you wonder how God would respond to such an honest and painful complaint? What follows is one of the Bible's most tender moments. God listens. He understands that they are men and women caught in time, easily losing perspective, losing hope that God is even paying attention. The Bible records:

And the LORD listened and heard them;
  So a book of remembrance was written
    before Him
For those who fear the LORD
  And who meditate on His name.

v. 16

Why is God writing a book of remembrance? To reassure His people that He does watch and care. And at a point in the future, He will reveal its contents. Read on:

"On the day that I make them My jewels....
  You shall again discern...

Between one who serves God
And one who does not serve Him."

vv. 17–18

What a picture of God's love and fairness! Whatever things might look like right now, on a day in the future, He will open His book of remembrance, and the truth about His generosity, faithfulness, and justice will be evident to all. Not one act of service in His name will have gone unnoticed or unrewarded.

As the roomful of believers at that retreat saw the truth, their discouragement fled. Some shed tears as they realized how much they'd underestimated their King. Many gladly recommitted themselves to His service. How could they not, they said, when He'd promised to one day make everything wonderfully right?

Before we closed that session, I showed them something else amazing in the Bible about that Day. Now I want to show you.

THE JESUS OF THE LAST PAGE

If you're a parent, you probably know that feeling of looking into your child's upturned face and realizing that you hold it in your power to make her biggest wish come true, *and then some!*

That's how Jesus feels about you right now.

Not one act of service in His name will have gone unnoticed.

You see, the message at the close of the Old Testament is repeated at the close of the New. If you turn to the last page of Revelation, you can read it. You'll find it in the final promise of Jesus:

"Behold, I am coming quickly, and My reward is with Me, to give to every one according to his work."

REVELATION 22:12

I'm struck by the fact that Jesus doesn't say, "I'm coming quickly to set up My kingdom." You see, He cares most about the *people* of His kingdom—people who have given a lifetime to Him because they believed what He said, and they wanted to please Him, and they chose to be faithful.

Do you see your God in a fresh light? He is a God who notices and cares about your every attempt, no matter how small, to serve Him. He sees your upturned face, knows your heart, and cares about your faithfulness.

He promises to reward you…and He can't wait to do so!

LIVING TOWARD YOUR "WELL DONE!"

I remember when Darlene Marie and I first chose to believe in God's eternal reward and to live for that Day. It dramatically changed our actions and priorities. It reordered how our family handled our money, our time, and our abilities. It added new, obvious urgency to how we tended to unfinished business. We became more grateful, more overwhelmed by the kindness of God.

And we began to live every day for the Rewarder's "Well done."

Since then, we've met hundreds of other men and women who, at Jesus' invitation, have looked into eternity and are now on an outrageous mission—to live for God's pleasure.

We became more grateful, more overwhelmed by the kindness of God.

They are wealthy business-men who have told us they "owned" nothing, not even their shoes. They are students who see an adventure for God in every new face, every difficult class and belittling job. They are young mothers who enthusias-tically serve a great King, realiz-ing that their most important work for all of eternity might be the little ones sleep-ing in the nursery or toddling down the hall.

These exuberant pilgrims seem a lot like other people on the surface, but they understand a day's pos-sibilities from a completely different point of view. Every day is a new opportunity to discover what eter-nal business might be lurking in the ordinary business of being human.

Sure, they are living *in* the dot, but they are living *for* the line. They're making a difference for God on the streets of New Delhi and Manchester and Lagos and Biloxi....

But they are already citizens of heaven.

CHANGE OF ADDRESS

Friend, I believe that God is asking you to make a life-changing decision before you leave this book. You need to change your citizenship from earth to heaven.

When Jesus was preparing to leave His disciples, He talked about that place. Listen to His words:

> *"In My Father's house are many mansions; if it were not so, I would have told you. I go to prepare a place for you. And if I go and prepare a place for you, I will come again and receive you to Myself; that where I am, there you may be also."*

JOHN 14:2–3

Think of all the ways Jesus could have described heaven. He could have talked about the streets of gold, the legions of angels, the thrones on which the apostles will sit.

But Jesus wanted His followers to know that heaven was first and foremost…*home.*

The apostle Paul, though he was proud to be both a Jew and a Roman citizen, purposefully chose to think of himself as a citizen of heaven, not of earth

(Philippians 3:20). It was a deep longing to be in heaven with his Lord that occupied his thoughts, shaped his values, and ordered the use of his time. The consequence of Paul's choice continues to impact the world for God today.

If you have heard and understood what Jesus revealed about a life God rewards, and if you're ready to make today count for eternity, I encourage you to join me in declaring your new citizenship:

> *Lord Jesus, I have listened carefully to what You said about my home. I believe You, and I can't wait to be there with You. I renounce my allegiance to this visible and fleeting world and pledge my allegiance to You, King of heaven. From this day on, I will live as a citizen of heaven, my true home. As Your faithful steward, I will take every gift, opportunity, and resource that You place in my hands and multiply it greatly for You. And I eagerly look forward to the day in eternity when I will stand in Your presence, and receive Your reward, and worship You forever.*

HOMECOMING

Picture your homecoming, the moment when all of eternity and all the angels and saints pause for you. Heaven will hush as you stand before your Savior to hear Him say, "Well done, good and faithful servant!" And then heaven will erupt with welcome and celebration as you accept the incorruptible crown that Jesus is reserving for you.

Heaven will erupt with welcome and celebration.

It will be your unique moment to bless the heart of God. On that day, you will prove that you valued Jesus' death for you, and you gave Him your heart and life in return.

God wants that day, when unseen and eternal things become visible, to be the most wonderful day of your life.

This book is a gift to you for that day, with great anticipation.

CHRISTIAN LEADERS
on ETERNAL REWARDS

JUSTIN MARTYR—*Even if we persuade only a few, we shall obtain very great rewards, for, like good laborers, we shall receive recompense from the Master.*

MARTIN LUTHER—*Now when Christ says: make to yourselves friends, lay up for yourselves treasures, and the like, you see that he means: do good, and it will follow of itself without your seeking, that you will have friends, find treasures in heaven, and receive a reward.*

JOHN WESLEY—*God will reward every one according to his works. But this is well consistent with his distributing advantages and opportunities of improvement, according to his own good pleasure.*

AUGUSTINE—*Therefore, we should seek from none other than the Lord God whatever it is that we hope to do well, or hope to obtain as reward for our good works.*

R. C. SPROUL—*There are degrees of reward that are given in heaven. I'm surprised that this answer surprises so many people. I think there's a reason Christians are shocked when I say there are various levels of heaven as well as graduations of severity of punishment in hell.*

JOHN CALVIN—*Nothing is clearer than that a reward is promised to good works, in order to support the weakness of our flesh by some comfort; but not to inflate our minds with vain glory.*

THEODORE H. EPP—*The primary purpose of the Judgment Seat of Christ is the examination of the lives and service of believers, and the rewarding of them for what God considers worthy of recognition.*

CHARLES R. SWINDOLL—*One of the great doctrines of Christianity is our firm belief in a heavenly home. Ultimately, we shall spend eternity with God in the place He has prepared for us. And part of that exciting anticipation is His promise to reward His servants for a job well done. I don't know many believers in Jesus Christ who never think of being with their Lord in heaven, receiving His smile of acceptance, and hearing His "Well done, good and faithful servant." We even refer to one who died in this way: "He has gone home to his reward."*

JONATHAN EDWARDS—*There are many mansions in God's house because heaven is intended for various degrees of honor and blessedness. Some are designed to sit in higher places there than others; some are designed to be advanced to higher degrees of honor and glory than others are; and, therefore, there are various mansions, and some more honorable mansions and seats, in heaven than others. Though they are all seats of exceeding honor and blessedness yet some more so than others.*

CHARLES H. SPURGEON—*Seek secrecy for your good deeds. Do not even see your own virtue. Hide from yourself that which you yourself have done that is commendable; for the proud contemplation of your own generosity may tarnish all your alms. Keep the thing so secret that even you yourself are hardly aware that you are doing anything at all praiseworthy. Let God be present, and you will have enough of an audience. He will reward you,* reward you "openly," reward you as a Father rewards a child, reward you as one who saw what you did, and knew that you did it wholly unto him.

JOHN MACARTHUR JR.—*There will be varying degrees of reward in heaven. That shouldn't surprise us: There are varying degrees of giftedness even here on earth.*

ORIGEN—*But if it was recorded that my Jesus was received up into glory, I perceive the divine arrangement in such an act, viz., because God, who brought this to pass, commends in this way the Teacher to those who witnessed it, in order that as men who are contending not for human doctrine, but for divine teaching, they may devote themselves as far as possible to the God who is over all, and may do all things in order to please Him, as those who are to receive in the divine judgment the reward of the good or evil which they have wrought in this life.*

CHARLES R. SWINDOLL—*He is waiting to welcome us. To those who serve, to those who stand where Jesus Christ once stood many, many years ago, He promises a reward. And we can be sure He will keep His promise.*

JOHN WESLEY—*Of those who had happily finished their course, such multitudes are afterwards described, and still higher degrees of glory which they attain after a sharp fight and magnificent victory, Rev. 14:1; 15:2; 19:1; 20:4. There is an inconceivable variety in the degrees of reward in the other world. Let not any slothful one say, "If I get to heaven at all, I will be content!" Such a one may let heaven go altogether. In worldly things, men are ambitious to get as high as they can. Christians have a far more noble ambition. The difference between the very highest and the lowest* state in the world is nothing to the smallest difference between the degrees of glory.

CLEMENT OF ALEXANDRIA—*And you know that, of all truths, this is the truest, that the good and godly shall obtain the good reward inasmuch as they held goodness in high esteem; while, on the other hand, the wicked shall receive meet punishment.*

DWIGHT L. MOODY—*If we are Christ's, we are here to shine for Him: by and by He will call us home to our reward.*

JOHN CALVIN—*Conversely, when we see the righteous brought into affliction by the ungodly, assailed with injuries, overwhelmed with calumnies, and lacerated by insult and contumely, while, on the contrary, the wicked flourish, prosper, acquire ease and honour, and all these with impunity, we ought forthwith to infer that there will be a future life in which iniquity shall receive its punishment, and righteousness its reward.*

R. C. SPROUL—*Saint Augustine said that it's only by the grace of God that we ever do anything even approximating a good work, and none of our works are good enough to demand that God reward them. The fact that God has decided to grant rewards on the basis of obedience or disobedience is what Augustine called God's crowning his own works within us. If a person has been faithful in many things through many years, then he will be acknowledged by His Master, who will say to him, "Well done, thou good and faithful servant." The one who squeaks in at the last minute has precious little good works for which he can expect reward.*

THEODORE H. EPP—*God is eager to reward us and does everything possible to help us lay up rewards. But if we are slothful* and carnal, so that our service counts for nothing, we shall be saved, yet so as by fire. Let us determine by the grace of God not to be empty handed when we stand before the bema, the Judgment Seat of Christ.

MARTIN LUTHER—*Therefore, he who does good works and guards himself against sin, God will reward.*

C. S. LEWIS—*If there lurks in most modern minds the notion that to desire our own good and earnestly to hope for the enjoyment of it is a bad thing, I submit that this notion has crept in from Kant and the Stoics and is not part of the Christian faith. Indeed, if we consider the unblushing promises of reward and the staggering nature of the rewards promised in the Gospels, it would seem that Our Lord finds our desires not too strong, but too weak.*

JOHN WESLEY—*For a man cannot profit God. Happy is he who judges himself an unprofitable servant; miserable is he whom God pronounces such. But though we are unprofitable to him, our serving him is not unprofitable to us; for he is pleased to give by his grace a value to our good works which, in consequence of his promise, entitles us to an eternal reward.*

JOHN CALVIN—*Thus Paul enjoins servants, faithfully doing what is of their duty, to hope for recompense from the Lord, but he adds "of the inheritance" (Colossians 3:24).*

R. C. SPROUL—*I'd say there are at least twenty-five occasions where the New Testament clearly teaches that we will be granted rewards according to our works. Jesus frequently holds out the reward motif as the carrot in front of the horse—"great will be your reward in heaven" if you do this or that. We are called to work, to store up treasures for ourselves in heaven, even as the* *wicked, as Paul tells us in Romans, "treasure up wrath against the day of wrath."*

CHARLES R. SWINDOLL—*On top of these temporal benefits connected to serving, there are eternal rewards as well. Christ Himself, while preparing the Twelve for a lifetime of serving others, promised an eternal reward even for holding out a cup of cool water.*

BILLY GRAHAM—*The believer has his foundation in Jesus Christ. Now we are to build upon this foundation, and the work we have done must stand the ultimate test; final exams come at the Judgment Seat of Christ when we receive our rewards.*

CHARLES STANLEY—*The kingdom of God will not be the same for all believers. Let me put it another way. Some believers will have rewards for their earthly faithfulness; others will not. Some will reign with Christ; others will not (see 2 Tim. 2:12). Some will be rich in the kingdom of God; others will be poor (see Luke 12:21, 33). Some will be given true riches; others will not (see Luke 16:11). Some will be given heavenly treasures of their own; others will not (see Luke 16:12).*

NOTES

CHAPTER 2

Randy Alcorn uses the Dot and Line illustration in his book *The Treasure Principle* (Sisters, Ore.: Multnomah Publishers, 2001).

SOURCES FOR CHRISTIAN LEADERS ON ETERNAL REWARDS

R. C. Sproul quotes excerpted from *Now, That's a Good Question!* by R. C. Sproul © 1996. Used by permission of Tyndale House Publishers, Inc. All rights reserved.

John MacArthur Jr. quote taken from "Bible Questions and Answers," GC 70-13, 1992, cassette. Source: www.biblebb.com/files/macqa/70-13-5.htm. Used by permission.

Theodore H. Epp quotes taken from *Present Labor and Future Rewards* by Theodore H. Epp (Lincoln, Neb.: Back to the Bible, 1960), 78, 86. Used by permission.

C. S. Lewis quote taken from *The Weight of Glory* by C. S. Lewis copyright © C. S. Lewis Pte. Ltd. 1949. Extract reprinted by permission.

Charles Stanley quote reprinted by permission of Thomas Nelson Publishers from the book entitled *Eternal Security* © 1990 by Charles Stanley.

Charles R. Swindoll quotes from *Improving Your Serve* by Charles R. Swindoll © 1981 W Publishing Group, Nashville, Tennessee. All rights reserved.

Billy Graham quote from *Facing Death and the Life After* by Billy Graham © 1987, W Publishing Group, Nashville, Tennessee. All rights reserved.

New companion products for
A Life God Rewards™

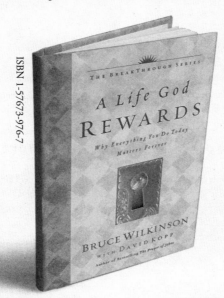

ISBN 1-57673-976-7

THE BREAKTHROUGH SERIES

A Life God
REWARDS
Why Everything You Do Today Matters Forever

BRUCE WILKINSON
WITH DAVID KOPP
Author of Bestselling The Prayer of Jabez

God Rewards His Kids

Board Book for Little Ones
ISBN 1-59052-094-7

Specially Illustrated for Kids
ISBN 1-59052-095-5

Begin an Eternal Adventure

Girls Only (Ages 9–12)
ISBN 1-59052-097-1

90-Day Challenge Devotional
ISBN 1-59052-099-8

Guys Only (Ages 9–12)
ISBN 1-59052-096-3

90-Day Challenge Devotional
ISBN 1-59052-098-X

Straight Talk to Teens about Eternity

A Life God Rewards for Teens
ISBN 1-59052-077-7

The BreakThrough Series, Books One and Two

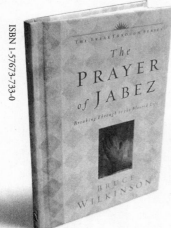

ISBN 1-57673-733-0

"Fastest selling book of all time."
—*Publishers Weekly*

- #1 *New York Times* Bestseller
- Over 9 Million Sold!
- 2001 & 2002 Gold Medallion Book of the Year

ISBN 1-57673-975-9

- *New York Times* Bestseller
- Over 3 Million Sold!